A Rock Is My Brother

A Rock Is My Brother

―――――∽∞∽―――――

Ron Mills

Illustrated by Jim Padgett

Abingdon Press
Nashville

A Rock Is My Brother

Copyright © 1998 by Abingdon Press

All rights reserved

No part of this work may be reproduced or transmitted in any form or by any means, electronic or mechanical, including photocopying and recording, or by any information storage or retrieval system, except as may be expressly permitted by the 1976 Copyright Act or in writing from the publisher.. Requests for permission should be addressed to Abingdon Press, 201 Eighth Avenue, South, P.O. Box 801, Nashville, TN 37202-0801.

This book is printed on recycled, acid-free paper..

ISBN 0-687-084385

Book design by Corky Lavin

98 99 00 01 02 03 04 05 06 07 — 10 9 8 7 6 5 4 3 2 1

MANUFACTURED IN THE UNITED STATES OF AMERICA

CONTENTS

A Rock Is My Brother
Page 6

Love in a Wet Foot
Page 16

Resurrection Rock
Page 24

Dancing Lessons
Page 34

Two Days Journey to the World
Page 42

A Rock Is My Brother

"It would be easier, Simon, if you pulled your side of the net when I pulled mine," I said.

"Look!" my brother motioned toward the lone figure circling the lake shore.

"I would rather pull nets," I replied.

Half of the day stretched out behind us. We had little to show for our efforts. Even a bad day on the water, though, calls for wonder. Bright green rolls off Galilee's hills tumbling into the olive brown lake. The sky drapes the landscape in clear blue.

A breeze brushes coolly against the skin on the hottest of days, carrying the subtle fragrance of wildflowers even as it buoys the gulls silently overhead. Yes, even on a bad fish day, the rhythmic lap and sway of water beneath the boat soothes the soul. The greenness, the air, the sky, the blue water of Galilee, hold my life in a pleasant place. It held my ancestors too. Its beauty keeps the soul pointed toward God.

"He's motioning to us," Simon said. The stranger stood at the shore, waving his hands over his head.

"Do you know him?" I asked.

"I heard him near the market in Capernaum a few days ago," he answered.

"What does he want? Did you know he was coming?"

"No, and I do not know what he wants," my brother answered.
"But we will find out."
Simon waved his hand

A Rock Is My Brother

overhead letting the stranger know we saw his gesture. We pulled in the last of the dripping nets. A small catch spilled into the boat. Simon centered himself between the oars and began the strokes that would take us to shore. The stranger stood calmly. Sometimes he looked at us. At other times he gazed beyond us.

"Who is he, Simon?" I asked with rising curiosity.

"I do not know him really," my brother answered. "I listened to him speaking to a small group near the market in Capernaum. "I tell you, Andrew; I never heard words like his, not even from the scribes.

A Rock Is My Brother

My heart blazed at some of his words about God. At one point he looked deeply into my eyes. I sat transfixed. I felt as if our spirits mingled and I understood a deep purpose in his life. His words, Andrew, are like no one else's. They reach the very place where the soul listens."

My brother's words astounded me. I knew how he looked into the heart of a person. I glanced warily back at the stranger. I held him in respect because of my brother, though I had never met the man.

"Simon," the man said as we dragged the boat to the sandy shore, "it is time now to begin a new thing. Come! Be a part of what God is doing. Come! Follow me, you and your brother." I glanced quickly at my brother. He did not move. He stared silently into the stranger's eyes. The expression on my brother's face told me deep within him something was happening. He surprised me only a little when he said to the man, "I will." Then, though I did not understand completely what I was doing, I said the same thing!

Explaining our decision to our family and friends proved impossible. We tried. No one understood why we would even consider such an undertaking with someone we did not know. Finally, we gave

up trying to explain and focused on making our preparations to follow this man Jesus. Many questions ran through my mind. How would we live? What would become of our fishing business? When the journey with this unfamiliar Jesus had run its course, would anything remain to rebuild our lives? These questions would have overwhelmed me except for the flicker in my heart telling me this would be no ordinary adventure. The strength of my brother's conviction helped me. His certainty gave me a place upon which to build my own. So we left to follow this man, traveling with fragile certainty and burning hearts.

A Rock Is My Brother

Our hearts proved reliable. As we traveled with Jesus, I grew confident that he would lead us into a new understanding of God and of ourselves. Others, besides Simon and myself, joined him. Twelve of us in all. Jesus seemed purposeful in gathering twelve of us. Oh, he permitted anyone to follow him, but he had a special relationship with us. 'The Twelve' he called us. We were with him constantly, except for moments he withdrew from us and went to be alone to pray.

Jesus' magnetism and his teaching attracted crowds wherever we traveled. His touch healed many who were sick. He seemed wiser than the religious leaders. The common people loved him. I felt privileged to follow him, though I often wondered why Jesus desired to be with such ordinary people.

One day, after much walking, we sat wearily as the fire crackled beneath a rack of fish. "Who do the people say that I am?" Jesus said to no one in particular.

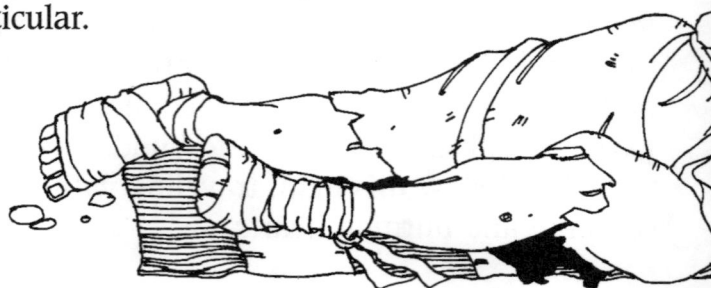

It would have been difficult to travel with Jesus and not hear the opinions about him. Once people heard him speak, they inevitably compared him to the greatest of teachers and rabbis. You could hear the word "prophet" whispered. Some went further and referred to Jesus as the great prophet Elijah. Others said John the Baptist had returned in Jesus. We ran through all the comments we heard. Everyone realized Jesus was more than just a traveling teacher, but no one was really certain. No one really knew that much about him.

"And you," the master asked, "who do you say I am?"

A moment later my brother blurted out, "You are the Messiah, the Son of the Living God."

A Rock Is My Brother

None of the rest of us thought along those lines, really. I figured my brother was off on another of his hasty exclamations. I was ready to correct him when Jesus said to him, "Simon, you did not come to this understanding on your own, but my Father in heaven revealed this to you."

Then Jesus did the most amazing thing. "You are Peter!" he said to my brother. Jesus' words fascinated me. He just named my brother the common word for rock. Jesus gave Simon a new name!

"You are Peter, and on this rock I will build my church."

Of course none of us understood what was happening at this point, even Simon; I mean, Peter. He sat looking at Jesus. He looked around at us. Questions danced in everybody's eyes. Yet, we shared the sense that Jesus communicated something deep to Peter and to us. We witnessed Peter's new name. Jesus wanted it that way. Though things were not clear in this present moment, I sensed they would become so later. The master clearly was laying the groundwork for something for the future. He would build upon my brother's confession of Jesus as Messiah, the Son of God. Now I would have to get used to this new name, Peter. It tickles me. A rock is my brother!

A Rock Is My Brother

Peter motioned toward the basin and pitcher. "It's not my turn, Peter!" I said to my brother wearily. I pointed to James and John. "How about one of the Zebedees? They haven't done anything lately." I thought this day would not end. We had traveled from Bethany, where Mary, Martha, and their brother, Lazarus, lived. We were journeying to Jerusalem for the Passover. All the attention slowed us down and made our own journey more tedious.

Then, the journey grew more hectic. Some of the crowd began to cut tree branches. They waved them over their heads shouting, "Hosanna." Jesus surprised us by selecting a young donkey and riding it into Jerusalem. The crowd wanted to celebrate and Jesus seemed content to let them. I could not understand everything. Neither could the rest of the Twelve.

Love in a Wet Foot

Along the way and even in Jerusalem, Jesus taught as if he were running out of time. We arrived at the room as the daylight waned. Outside, people moved on the street, talking. I relaxed easily as I listened to the street sounds. I felt tired, yet relieved to be away from the noisy crowd.

Somebody else can do it this time, I thought. No one made a move. I wondered if we were thinking the same thing. It seemed a good time to skip the washing, although all of us wanted our feet cleansed. Water at day's end refreshed a person. It lightened the day. A little of the weariness washed off with the dust of the road. We simply wanted somebody else to do the washing. Sitting felt too good.

We were engaged in conversation about the day when Jesus walked over to the basin. I waited for him to ask one of us to do the task. Instead,

Jesus, without saying a word, took off his outer garment. He took the towel lying near the basin and wrapped it around himself.

"What is he doing?" I whispered to Peter.

By that time all twelve of us had noticed Jesus' actions. Silence spread throughout the room. Wordlessly, we watched our teacher stoop down. He gently took a foot and drizzled water over it. After washing it, he dried it with a towel. One by one the master worked his way around the noiseless room.

Love in a Wet Foot

Peter shifted tensely in his chair. His discomfort with Jesus' actions appeared on his face. Jesus knelt before my brother. Peter's restlessness exploded with, "Not my feet, Lord! You are not going to wash my feet!" The words shattered the tension in the air. What he said was in all of our hearts though. Of course, the silence in the room before my brother's outburst was nothing compared to the silence now. Jesus stopped his actions. He looked into Peter's eyes. "If I do not wash you, you have no part in me."

Jesus grew still. His attention fixed on Peter. The rest of us waited, almost afraid to breathe, for my brother's response. Whatever we thought Jesus was doing with the towel and the basin changed in that instant. Our master performed something more than the familiar act of hospitality. We realized we had entered again a deeper realm of God's life. Jesus continually led us to those regions.

Obviously my brother did not completely understand Jesus' words. He comprehended enough though. He said quickly, "Then Lord, not my feet only, but also my hands and my head." Jesus seemed to look for the willingness to follow him. Understanding would come. My brother knew

that. He belonged to Jesus. He extended his feet to the master.

Later, Jesus put away the towel and the basin. He turned to us and asked, "Do you know what I have done for you?"

No one answered.

"I, your Lord and teacher, have washed your feet. I have taken the time to serve you, to refresh you. You ought to do that for one another. Treat each other the way I have treated you. I am giving you a new commandment now. Love one another as I have loved you. The world will know you have been with me. It will know you are following me if you love one another."

Love in a Wet Foot

Peter leaned back against the wall in thoughtfulness. All of us were pondering what had happened. Really, Jesus left us in a constant state of ponder. Never have I thought so much about life or about God before I met him.

"We seem so selfish, don't we, brother?" Peter said to me. "We sat around, all of us, waiting for someone else to serve us. We did not want to take the initiative. We did not want to care for others. Jesus asks us to think about how we can help another person instead of waiting to be helped. He leads us into places so foreign to our heart. When we arrive there, God seems to be waiting for us. I am beginning to see, Andrew, how much people matter to God. God wants more than our religion. People matter. The love we show to others may be

the very bridge we travel away from ourselves into God!"

This was my brother the fisherman talking! Sometimes I could not believe the things coming out of his mouth. Sometimes he spoke too quickly. Sometimes he completely missed the point. At other times though, I knew that Peter was saying something solid, something eternal. He spoke words persons who longed for God could build their faith on. I had just heard such words.

Resurrection Rock

The sight of a Roman soldier coming toward me unnerved me. Apprehension quickly changed to joy when I recognized his face. "Gaius!" I said, seeing my old friend from Capernaum.

"I am sorry about your master," Gaius said. "He did not deserve to die in such a shameful way."

"None of us can explain it," I replied. "We could never have predicted this end after traveling with

A Rock Is My Brother

Jesus. His words were the very words of life itself. His death leaves creation speechless."

"A horrible loss," Gaius said compassionately. "I came upon Simon, weeping bitterly outside Caiaphas' house last evening. I could not console him."

"He is going by a new name now," I told my friend. "Jesus named him Peter."

"Rock?" Gaius replied curiously.

"Yes," I continued, motioning toward Peter. "Behold the rock on which Jesus was to build his new community."

We looked toward the far end of the room. Peter had stationed himself at the window. My brother had been staring for hours into the night. He had

Resurrection Rock

not eaten in more than a day. He did not acknowledge Gaius' presence in the room at all.

"His grief moves within him like poison, Gaius," I said after a brief pause. "You know Peter has never been one to hold his tongue. Not long ago he proclaimed loudly that he would follow Jesus anywhere, even to the point of laying down his life for him. In the end, out of fear, he denied he even knew Jesus. He ran away like the rest of us. Denial tortures him even as sadness breaks him. You can mix some confusion into his heart too."

"What do you mean?" Gaius asked.

"Mary brought Peter word this morning that the tomb was empty. She received word from an angelic messenger that Jesus was alive! Peter went to the tomb and found it just like Mary said. It's so unbelievable. Mary's message was that Jesus would meet us in Galilee. You can see though, Peter's sadness throbs full force."

"You should return to Galilee," Gaius said. "Guards will be searching house to house for you. Go as quickly as you can." He stood to leave, "Take care of yourselves, my friends."

Not long after Gaius left, the other members of the Twelve arrived at the room. We locked the doors and sunk into the evening's chaos.

Resurrection Rock

We made plans for the journey back to Galilee. I don't remember who was the first one to see him. His presence startled us all. Jesus, the crucified one, stood among us. "Peace be with you!" he said. We looked nervously at each other, then at our master. How could we believe what we were seeing! No mistaking it though. Wounds in his hands and his feet! We were in the presence of our Lord! "Peace be with you," Jesus said again.
He was sending us now, he told us, just as God had sent him. Jesus breathed on us, "Receive the Holy Spirit." Things happened quickly. We tried talking all at once. Jesus vanished. He left us buzzing with questions. A strange peace pushed the fear out of my heart. I remained confused, but I felt the sadness leave me. In its place came an unexplainable confidence. The adventure with Jesus continued.

The others felt it too. Even Peter.

We talked excitedly on our way back to Galilee. What direction should our lives take since Jesus had appeared to us? We were not sure. We decided to take up fishing again until things grew clearer. James, John, Peter, a few other disciples, and I raised money among ourselves. We bought a small boat and outfitted it. We guided the boat out into the night waters of the Sea of Galilee. We were either out of practice or out of rhythm. We caught absolutely nothing. We tried all night.

At daybreak, we tired and headed to shore. Someone called to us, "You have no fish have you."

"No," we all said, looking at the stranger at the shore.

"Cast the net on the right side of the boat. You will find some," the stranger said.

"This is crazy," Peter said. "We've cast nets all night. I say we pull in and head to shore."

"Wait, Peter," I said. "I remember another time a stranger called to us from this same shore. Although I cannot explain my reasons, let's do as he says."

"Aww, Andrew," my brother said.

We threw the nets to the right side of the boat. Immediately, we felt the weight of a huge catch. Four of us pulled with all our strength. Great drops of sweat poured off our foreheads. John stopped pulling and stared at the man on the shore. Then, John's face glowed. "It is the Lord!" he said. Before the words left John's mouth, my brother lunged into Galilee's water. We dragged the boat ashore. Peter met us excitedly. We smelled the fire. My brother retrieved some of the fish we caught, and

prepared them for the fire.

After breakfast, we sat around the fire still amazed at our master's presence with us. Jesus asked my brother if he loved him.

"You know I love you," Peter replied.

"Feed my lambs," Jesus answered him.

Jesus gestured with his hands toward us when he said that. It seemed he was asking Peter to take care of us. Again Jesus asked my brother if he loved him.

"Yes, Lord, you know I love you," came my brother's quick reply.

"Tend my sheep," Jesus returned.

I could see the questions in my brother's eyes. All of us looked around at each other. We tried to make sense out of Jesus' questions. Again the

Resurrection Rock 31

same query, "Peter, do you love me?"

Well, by now Peter was frustrated at having the same question asked to him three times.

"Lord, you know everything, you know I love you," Peter said, trying desperately to discover what Jesus wanted him to say.

"Feed my sheep," our master said.

"You know, Andrew," my brother said to me as we walked along many years after that breakfast, "I still carry Jesus' questions in my heart. Look how the little flock of Jesus has grown. I cannot see what we will become. We will always need care though. That is what Jesus asked me to do that

day, to care. It's amazing. Jesus named me "Rock." I denied him and ran away afraid. He never abandoned me. The name Jesus gave me became a truth that kept me through all my failings.

"Jesus saw your strength from the very beginning, Peter," I said.

"Jesus has been our strength from the very beginning," Peter said.

I put my hand on the shoulder of my brother, the Rock. I thanked God again for what Jesus had done in both of our lives.

Resurrection Rock

Dancing Lessons

A Rock Is My Brother

Jesus' resurrection breakfast changed our plans immediately. We sold the fishing boat we acquired. We needed no more time to discover the direction of the master's call. We were to tell other persons about Jesus and God's mighty acts through him. God would take care of us. People were hungry for the good news we preached. They responded with praise and worship and a generous sharing of their goods. The fellowship of believers grew quite large.

The spirit of Jesus grew strong in my brother. He fed the people daily with his teaching and preaching. He tended the growing numbers of believers. He responded to the needs the growing community created. The preaching about Jesus created something like a new family. Everyone enjoyed being together in Jesus' name. One day the power of faith in Jesus' name amazed us all.

Dancing Lessons

It was the hour of afternoon prayers. Peter and John and I approached the Temple. Today we were coming up into the gate named Beautiful. I could see in the distance the beggars in their places. Other unfortunate ones arrived ahead of the crowds coming for prayer. Two persons carried one poor soul. I watched them lay him down near the gate.

The three of us made our way with others to the Temple area. I reached in the small bag I carried with me. I placed my last coin into the cloak of a man who was blind. When we arrived at the Temple gate, the man I had seen earlier being carried called out to Peter for alms. Peter looked at John.

"Do you have any coins left?" he asked John.

"No," John replied.

"Andrew?" my brother asked.

"None," I said. "I just gave my last away a few steps back."

Peter stopped before the man who was lame. "Look at us," he said to the man.

The man stopped asking for alms from everyone. He turned his expectant gaze to my brother. He held out his hand for what he thought would be a few coins. I watched the two of them staring at each other for a moment. Although I did not know what, I knew something was about to happen. Peter said to the man, "I do not have silver or gold to give you. I will give you what I have."

I looked at John. He was as baffled as I was at what my brother was doing. Peter then reached down and took the startled man's right hand. "In the name of Jesus Christ of Nazareth, walk!"

My eyes bulged with astonishment. I glanced quickly at John. He stared wide-eyed at Peter. Peter was raising the man, clearly frightened now, up off the ground. I did not know whether to help my brother raise the man who was lame or to persuade

Dancing Lessons

my brother to place him gently back down again. Suddenly, the man's expression changed dramatically from fear to something like a bewildered joy. Peter relaxed his grip. He was not lifting dead weight now. The man's own strength supported him. "My legs!" he screamed joyfully, looking at Peter then at John and me.

I backed away, astounded at what I witnessed. John fell on his knees. Peter released the man's hand completely. The man stood for the first time in his life. He gazed around at the those who had stopped when they saw what was happening. He squatted down then stood again.

He twirled around with an incredible smile on his face. He jumped high up into the air, ran a few steps and jumped again.

"God has healed me!" he shouted. He grabbed one bystander, then another, and another.

"God be praised for Jesus Christ of Nazareth!" the man proclaimed in gratitude to God.

Peter, John, and I watched the happy man dance and leap and startle passersby with his glee. We turned to enter the Temple area. *What an astonishing God we have,* I thought.

"Wait, wait for me!" the man shouted when he saw us turn to go. "I'll go with you to the Temple. I have enough joy to fill Jerusalem!" We walked through the Temple grounds. I delighted in seeing the startled expression of persons who recognized this man. They knew he used to lie by the gate begging for alms. Everyone was speechless. Everyone, that is, except the healed man who kept dancing and leaping and praising God. I could not keep my mind off the miracle through the time of prayer.

"I'm curious, Peter," I said to my brother as we walked away from the Temple after prayer. "How did you know God would do such a miracle?"

"I did not know," my brother replied. "I simply wanted to give the man a few coins. As I drew closer to him, the presence of Jesus rose up inside me. I heard his voice saying, 'Peter, do you love me? Tend my sheep.' So I just did the first thing that came to my heart."

"Amazing!" I exclaimed.

My brother put his arm on my shoulder as we walked. "Andrew," he said, "the name of Jesus can make the lame dance! His name can change the world!"

"I don't doubt that brother," I said. "But the hard part is knowing when miraculous power will come."

"That's just it, Andrew," Peter said. "All the power of Jesus is present in human hands reaching to help someone in his name. Love is the power of God."

Dancing Lessons

Two Days Journey to the World

"You just missed him, Andrew," the tanner said. "He left this morning. And he left with Gentiles."

"Gentiles!" I said, surprised.

"A centurion sent them," he said. "Come in. Rest yourself."

As my friend went to retrieve a drink, I turned my gaze to the blue Mediterranean water. I loved Joppa. The constant sea breezes and the large expanse of shoreline made my soul expand.

"A few Romans arrived yesterday afternoon," the tanner said reentering the room. "From what I could gather, their centurion had been instructed to send the men here and bring your brother back with them."

"And my brother went with them?" I asked incredulously.

"Well, there's more to it," the tanner replied. "Yesterday about noon your brother went up to the housetop to pray. We were preparing some food here. It took longer than I thought it would. Next thing I know, Peter is down here. His face looks like a big question mark. It turns out he has had a vision. He told it to me, but I could not make sense of it. While we were talking about his vision, the

Two Days Journey to the World

men appeared, telling Peter about Cornelius. Peter sensed that he should go with them, although he could not say why exactly. He asked the men to stay for the night. They left this morning headed for Caesarea. Perhaps if you hurry you can catch them at the inn beyond Appollonia."

Peter and I stayed at the inn on an earlier journey to buy fishing supplies. Maybe they would stop there. I thanked my friend for his hospitality and headed north to Caesarea.

In the village of Appollonia, I inquired in the market about my brother and the believers who traveled with him from Joppa. The Roman soldiers escorting them would have made a memorable group. They had indeed passed through the village not long ago, the cloth merchant told me.

As the daylight began its evening spiral into a soft red glow, the air cooled. I quickened my pace. By the time I reached the inn, darkness made traveling difficult. I approached the lodging. I could hear the sound of Peter's voice among the others. "Andrew!" my brother said, as I pushed open the door. He stood, walked over to me and embraced me. "This is my brother," Peter said to the Romans. They offered me some wine and bread. The innkeeper placed cheese and fruit on the table. I was hungry. It had been a long day. I engaged in a little conversation. Soon the weariness overtook me, and I stretched out in my bed for the night.

During the next day's journey, my brother and I attempted to make sense of his vision and why he felt he should travel with these Romans.

"The very things we have been forbidden to touch or eat since our youth, the voice of God urged me to touch and eat," Peter said. We walked on in our perplexity until Stratos Tower came into view in the distance. "Ah, Caesarea," I sighed.

Two Days Journey to the World

Cornelius was waiting. The soldiers traveling with us escorted us into the room and introduced us. The centurion had called together his family and some of his close friends. Cornelius walked to meet us, then fell at Peter's feet. His actions took us by surprise. Peter placed a hand on the centurion's shoulder, bidding him to rise. "I am just an ordinary man," he told Cornelius. "Stand up." Peter looked at the people gathered. He said to them, "All of you know Jews don't associate with people from other nations. Yet God is showing me something new. You have asked me to come here. And I have come quickly. Now why did you bring me here?"

Cornelius returned to his seat and motioned for Peter to sit beside him. "I was praying about four days ago, Peter. About this very hour, a man stood before me. His clothes shone brightly. He said to me, 'Cornelius, your prayer has been heard. Your gifts to the poor have been remembered before God. Send to Joppa and ask for Peter.' So that is what I have done. We are present to hear everything you have been given by the Lord to say to us."

My brother turned to the room full of listeners. "I understand now the story of what God is doing in Jesus Christ is for a much larger audience than my people, the Jews. God has no favorites. Any person who believes in God and seeks to do what is right is welcomed into God's kingdom."

So my brother told them all about the love of God that came to us in Jesus of Nazareth. I watched their hearts melt in praise and glory to God. I felt my own heart warm. I realized Jesus was changing the whole world with his life. What Jesus had said many years ago was true. My brother and I and the rest of the disciples had become fishers of people. People who wanted to know the true God responded to our preaching. Jesus was building a great community of people.

In awe I watched the Gentiles worship. My brother was just an ordinary man sharing his faith in Jesus. I was there when he began the journey with the master. I listened to him sputter his new name, Peter, Rock. I watched my strong brother awkwardly handle the gentle servanthood the master taught us. I listened to Peter believe fervently in Jesus as Lord, then deny Jesus vehemently when fear got the best of him. I entered with him into his broken guilt. I leaped with him in the joyful discovery of Jesus' resurrection. I saw Peter tending Jesus' sheep. With open mouth I watched the healing power of God emerge from my brother's faith in Jesus' name. Now I stood beside my brother as he took the beloved name of Jesus beyond the boundary of our people and spoke it into the world.

Each day opens upon a new territory for believing in God. One thing remains true. Wherever I travel with this "rock," Jesus builds his people. After all of these years it still makes me smile: *a rock is my brother*. Thank God!